Instant Passbook App Development for iOS How-to

Create and customize a Passbook Pass with the exciting new iOS features

Keith D. Moon

PUBLISHING

BIRMINGHAM - MUMBAI

Instant Passbook App Development for iOS How-to

First published: June 2013

Production Reference: 1170613

Published by Packt Publishing Ltd.
Livery Place
35 Livery Street
Birmingham B3 2PB, UK.

ISBN 978-1-84969-706-4

www.packtpub.com

Credits

Author
Keith D. Moon

Reviewer
Aodh Ó Lionáird

Acquisition Editor
Joanne Fitzpatrick

Comissioning Editor
Neha Nagwekar

Technical Editor
Vrinda Nitesh Bhosale

Project Coordinator
Sneha Modi

Proofreader
Linda Morris

Graphics
Abhinash Sahu

Production Coordinator
Conidon Miranda

Cover Work
Conidon Miranda

Cover Image
Manu Joseph

About the Author

Keith D. Moon is an award-winning mobile application developer who has worked with some of the largest music artists and brands to create engaging and personal mobile experiences.

Keith has worked with international brands, including the BBC, Expedia, O2, and Sony Music, using the latest technologies and development practices to create mobile apps that provide value for both the user and brand.

Thank you to my supportive and amazing wife, Faith, and to my family for always providing support and encouragement.

About the Reviewer

Aodh Ó Lionáird holds a B.Sc. degree in Software Development from the Cork Institute of Technology and an M.Sc. degree in Interactive Media from University College Cork, Ireland. He is currently working on mobile applications as a Senior Developer with the BBC in London.

www.PacktPub.com

Support files, eBooks, discount offers and more

You might want to visit www.PacktPub.com for support files and downloads related to your book.

Did you know that Packt offers eBook versions of every book published, with PDF and ePub files available? You can upgrade to the eBook version at www.PacktPub.com and as a print book customer, you are entitled to a discount on the eBook copy. Get in touch with us at service@packtpub.com for more details.

At www.PacktPub.com, you can also read a collection of free technical articles, sign up for a range of free newsletters and receive exclusive discounts and offers on Packt books and eBooks.

http://PacktLib.PacktPub.com

Do you need instant solutions to your IT questions? PacktLib is Packt's online digital book library. Here, you can access, read and search across Packt's entire library of books.

Why Subscribe?

- ▸ Fully searchable across every book published by Packt
- ▸ Copy and paste, print and bookmark content
- ▸ On demand and accessible via web browser

Free Access for Packt account holders

If you have an account with Packt at www.PacktPub.com, you can use this to access PacktLib today and view nine entirely free books. Simply use your login credentials for immediate access.

Table of Contents

Preface

Instant Passbook App Development for iOS How-to will get you up and running with Passbook, Apple's digital wallet, introduced in iOS. Passbook provides a way for users to collect and organize coupons, store cards, event tickets, and boarding passes, and your product or service can take advantage of this opportunity. This book will explain the Passbook infrastructure, lead you through creating your first Pass, covering delivering your Passes to users, and keeping them up-to-date.

What this book covers

Understanding Passbook (Simple) introduces you to Passbook. Apple's Passbook feature is a collection of technologies that come together to provide digital wallet functionality to the user. We will understand what Passbook consists of, from both the user and Pass creator perspective.

Setting up your environment (Simple) guides you through creating a Pass. Creating your first Pass will require cryptographic keys and certificates, managed through Apple's Developer Portal. You will be lead through this, preparing everything needed to create your first Pass.

Creating your Pass (Medium) covers all the elements that go into a Pass. You will be taken through the creation of a Pass from beginning to end.

Signing your Pass (Simple) explains how to digitally sign the Pass package content. To be accepted into the Passbook app, a Pass must be cryptographically signed with the developer's certificate. We will sign the newly created Pass with the certificate prepared from your Apple Developer account.

Delivering your Pass via e-mail (Medium) explores how Passes can be delivered as e-mails. Once created, your Pass needs to be delivered to your users. We will send an e-mail with your Pass attached, in a way that allows it to be opened directly into Passbook.

Delivering your Pass via a web link (Medium) shows you how to configure your web server to serve up Passes to your users. This will allow Passes to be delivered though links from your website.

Delivering your Pass via an app (Medium) shows how Passes can be delivered through a companion iOS app. We will use the PassKit framework available in iOS to present a Pass to the user in a companion app. From there the Pass can be added into the Passbook App.

Updating a Pass within the Passbook app (Advanced) will implement a REST API in Ruby that matches Apple's defined specification. This will allow Passes to be updated when circumstances change.

What you need for this book

- ▶ Mac OSX (version 10.8.2 or greater recommended)
- ▶ Git Version Control
- ▶ A web hosting service; for example, Heroku (http://www.heroku.com)
- ▶ An Apple iOS Developer account (http://developer.apple.com/ios)

Who this book is for

This book is intended for those looking to take advantage of Passbook, the latest feature in iOS. Readers with familiarity with the iOS platform and with programming concepts will get the most from this book. While you will be lead through each part of the process step-by-step, readers with experience in building and packaging apps for the iOS platform will find familiar concepts.

Conventions

In this book, you will find a number of styles of text that distinguish between different kinds of information. Here are some examples of these styles, and an explanation of their meaning.

Code words in text, database table names, folder names, filenames, file extensions, pathnames, dummy URLs, user input, and Twitter handles are shown as follows: "Pass files with the -pkpass file extension will open in a preview window."

A block of code is set as follows:

```
if (![PKPassLibraryisPassLibraryAvailable]) {
    NSLog(@"Passbook not available on this device");
    return;
}
```

Any command-line input or output is written as follows:

```
cd passbook_rails_example
bundle
```

New terms and **important words** are shown in bold. Words that you see on the screen, in menus or dialog boxes for example, appear in the text like this: "Clicking on the **Add to Passbook** button will place the Pass in the Passbook associated with the iCloud account set up in OSX system preferences".

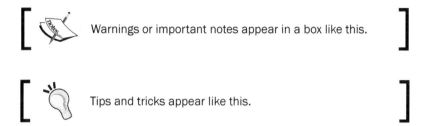

Warnings or important notes appear in a box like this.

Tips and tricks appear like this.

Reader feedback

Feedback from our readers is always welcome. Let us know what you think about this book—what you liked or may have disliked. Reader feedback is important for us to develop titles that you really get the most out of.

To send us general feedback, simply send an e-mail to feedback@packtpub.com, and mention the book title via the subject of your message.

If there is a topic that you have expertise in and you are interested in either writing or contributing to a book, see our author guide on www.packtpub.com/authors.

Customer support

Now that you are the proud owner of a Packt book, we have a number of things to help you to get the most from your purchase.

Downloading the example code

You can download the example code files for all Packt books you have purchased from your account at http://www.packtpub.com. If you purchased this book elsewhere, you can visit http://www.packtpub.com/support and register to have the files e-mailed directly to you.

Errata

Although we have taken every care to ensure the accuracy of our content, mistakes do happen. If you find a mistake in one of our books—maybe a mistake in the text or the code—we would be grateful if you would report this to us. By doing so, you can save other readers from frustration and help us improve subsequent versions of this book. If you find any errata, please report them by visiting http://www.packtpub.com/submit-errata, selecting your book, clicking on the **errata submission form** link, and entering the details of your errata. Once your errata are verified, your submission will be accepted and the errata will be uploaded on our website, or added to any list of existing errata, under the Errata section of that title. Any existing errata can be viewed by selecting your title from http://www.packtpub.com/support.

Piracy

Piracy of copyright material on the Internet is an ongoing problem across all media. At Packt, we take the protection of our copyright and licenses very seriously. If you come across any illegal copies of our works, in any form, on the Internet, please provide us with the location address or website name immediately so that we can pursue a remedy.

Please contact us at copyright@packtpub.com with a link to the suspected pirated material.

We appreciate your help in protecting our authors, and our ability to bring you valuable content.

Questions

You can contact us at questions@packtpub.com if you are having a problem with any aspect of the book, and we will do our best to address it.

Instant Passbook App Development for iOS How-to

Welcome to *Instant Passbook App Development for iOS How-to*. This book will guide you through creating a Passbook Pass, distributing it to your users, and integrating it in to your existing app.

Understanding Passbook (Simple)

This recipe will help you understand Passbook from the perspective of both, a user and a Pass creator.

Getting ready

With iOS, Apple introduced the Passbook app as a central digital wallet for all the store cards, coupons, boarding passes, and event tickets that have become a popular feature of apps.

A company wishing to take advantage of this digital wallet and the extra functionality it provides, can use Apple's developer platform to create a Pass for their users.

How to do it...

1. To understand Passbook, we need to see a Pass in action. Download the example Pass from:

   ```
   http://passkit.pro/example-generic-pkpass
   ```

2. If you open this link within Mobile Safari, on an iPhone or iPod Touch running iOS, you will be presented with the Pass and the option to add it to your Passbook:

3. Alternatively, you can download the Pass on a Mac or PC and e-mail it to yourself, and then open the e-mail within the Mail app on an iPhone or iPod Touch. Tapping the Pass attachment link will present the Pass.

4. If you choose to add the Pass to your Passbook app, the displayed Pass will disappear, having been filed away within your Passbook. Now, click on the **home** button to return to the home screen and launch the Passbook app. In the app you will now see the Pass that was just added. It contains information specified by the app creator and can be presented when interacting with the company providing the service. Additional information can be placed on the back of the Pass. Tap the **i** button in the top-right hand corner of the Pass, to reveal this information.

How it works...

The following diagram describes how Passes are delivered to a Passbook, and how these can be updated:

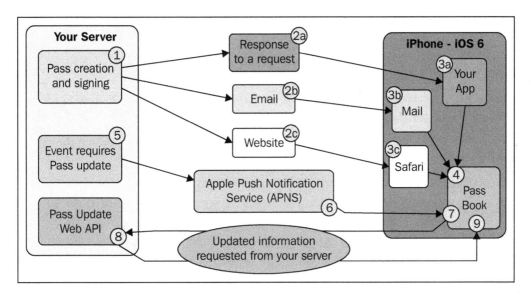

The process of creating a Pass involves cryptographically signing the Pass using a certificate and key generated from your iOS developer account. For this reason, the generation of the Pass needs to take place on a server, and then be delivered to Passbook either via your own app, as an e-mail attachment, or by embedding it in a website.

It's important to note that Apple does not provide any system for the Pass providers to authenticate, validate, or invalidate Passes. The Pass can contain barcode information, but it is up to the Pass provider to provide the infrastructure for reading and processing these barcodes.

Instead of just sitting in the Passbook app, waiting to be used, a Pass can contain location and time triggers, that proactively present the Pass to the user, serving as both a reminder and providing convenient access. For example, an event Pass could be set to appear 15 minutes before the start time, at the time when a user is likely to want to present their event Pass to an attendant. Alternatively, a coupon Pass could be presented as a user approaches their local store where the coupon can be redeemed.

Passes that have been added to Passbook can also be updated dynamically. For example, if the Pass is for a store card, a change to the card balance may require an update to the Pass. In the case of, for example an airline ticket Pass, a departure gate change should trigger a Pass update.

When a Pass needs to be updated, your server sends a **push notification** to the Passbook app on the user's device. This push notification is not displayed to the user.

Upon receiving this Push Notification, the Passbook app then makes a request to your server for the updated Pass information. Your server would then respond to the relevant request, and provide the updated information in the expected format.

When the Passbook App on the user's device receives the updated information, it silently updates the Pass. The next time the user looks at the Pass contained in the Passbook app, the updated information is displayed.

There's more...

Support for Passbook is also built into OSX Mountain Lion (10.8.2). Pass files with the pkpass file extension will open in a preview window:

Clicking on the **Add to Passbook** button will place the Pass in the Passbook associated with the iCloud account set up in OSX system preferences.

The OSX Mail app and Safari also support embedded Passes.

When building a Pass, you can specify a relevant time and up to 10 relevant locations that will trigger a message to be displayed on the lock screen. The message looks similar to a push notification, however a Pass notification is less intrusive. When it is relevant to display, it doesn't vibrate the iPhone and it doesn't wake up the screen. The notification only becomes visible when the phone wakes up from sleep:

The option to specify relevant times and locations, and how far from the location the notification is triggered, is determined by the Pass type, as we will see later.

Apps using Passbook

Some of the apps in the App Store using Passbook are as follows:

- **Hotels.com**: This uses Passbook for room reservation details. It can be downloaded from `http://appstore.com/hotelscom/hotelscom`.

- **Starbucks**: This uses Passbook for a store card. It can be downloaded from `http://appstore.com/starbuckscoffeecompany`.

- **Ticketmaster**: This uses Passbook for event tickets. It can be downloaded from `http://appstore.com/ticketmaster/ticketmaster`.

- **United Airlines**: This uses Passbook for boarding passes. It can be downloaded from `http://appstore.com/unitedairlines`.

Further documentation

For more details refer to Apple's Passbook documentation at `https://developer.apple.com/passbook/`.

Setting up your environment (Simple)

This recipe shows how to set up your Pass type in Apple's provisioning Portal and generate the required files for code signing.

Getting ready

To get started with creating your own Pass, you will need a paid iOS developer account. If you intend to present the Passes within an existing iOS app, you will need access to the iOS developer account that publishes this existing app. In addition, many of these steps require apps and utilities only available on OSX, Keychain Access for example, which is used in the certificate creation process. Therefore, these steps should be undertaken using a Mac, running OSX.

How to do it...

1. If you intend to present Passes within an iOS App, but have not yet created the app, you will need to create an App ID within the **Identifiers** section of the iOS Developer Center.

2. Log in to the iOS Developer Center and navigate to **Certificates | Identifiers & Profiles | Identifiers**, or follow this link:

   `https://developer.apple.com/account/ios/identifiers/bundle/bundleList.action`

3. Click the **+** button at the top-right hand corner.

4. Enter an app name in the **App ID Description** field:

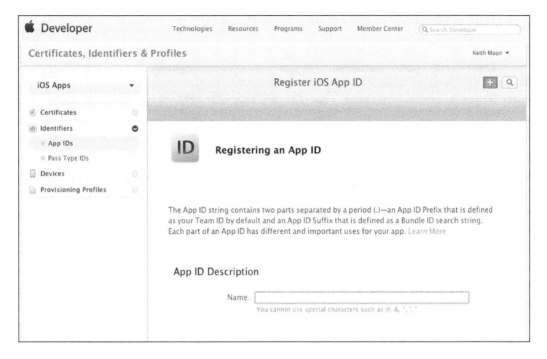

5. Under **Application Services**, ensure that **Passbook** is enabled.

6. Under **App ID Prefix**, use Team ID unless you have a reason to explicitly specify this.

7. An App ID Suffix is a string identifier that is unique to your app. The provisioning portal will not allow you to specify a Bundle Identifier being used in another app. The suggestion is to use a reverse domain name style string. For example, throughout this book I have used the domain name `http://passkit.pro`, therefore the Bundle Identifier I have chosen is `pro.passkit.example` as this will be the app ID for the example app.

8. If you have a pre-existing app ID, you will need to enable Passbook for this app ID. From the app ID section of the provisioning portal, select the app ID, and note down the prefix, as we need it when specifying the Team Identifier of your Pass. Having done this, choose **Settings**:

9. Check the checkbox next to Passbook and click on **Done**. A warning will be displayed, informing that all new provisioning profiles created for this app ID will be enabled for Passes. This is presented as a reminder that pre-existing provisioning profiles will not be enabled for Passbook, until they are re-created. Therefore, if you have a pre-existing App published to the App Store, you will need to re-generate the App's distribution provisioning profile, re-build the App with this new provisioning profile, and submit an update of the App to the App Store. Until you do this, your App will not be able to add Passes into Passbook. When Passes have been correctly enabled for an app ID the Passes' indicator will turn green and be labeled as **Enabled** in the app ID summary screen:

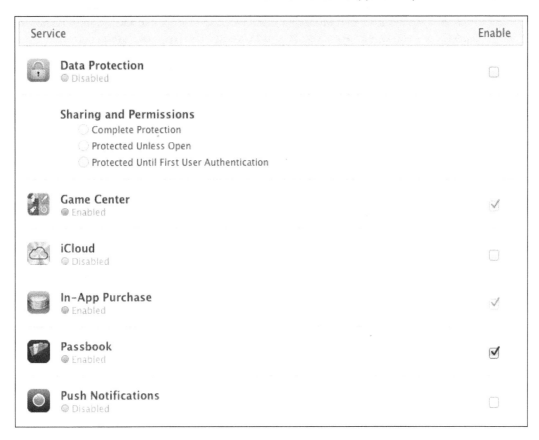

Service	Enable
Data Protection ◉ Disabled	☐
Sharing and Permissions ○ Complete Protection ○ Protected Unless Open ○ Protected Until First User Authentication	
Game Center ◉ Enabled	☑
iCloud ◉ Disabled	☐
In-App Purchase ◉ Enabled	☑
Passbook ◉ Enabled	☑
Push Notifications ◉ Disabled	☐

10. Regardless of whether you intend to present your Pass in an app, you will now need to create a Pass Type ID. Follow the link on the left menu for Pass Type IDs or visit:

    ```
    https://developer.apple.com/account/ios/identifiers/passTypeId/
    passTypeIdList.action
    ```

11. Click on the **+** button to create a new Pass Type ID. You will need to create a Pass Type ID for each type of Pass you intend to create. The types of Passes currently available to create are Boarding Pass, Coupon, Event Ticket, Store Card, and Generic. The Pass types are presented differently and have different functionality, as we will see. In our examples we will focus on building a Generic Pass. If you intend to create a Store Card type Pass and a Coupon type Pass, you will need to create a Pass Type ID for each:

12. For the description, choose a name that defines the type of Pass you are creating. For the main example later in the book, a Generic type Pass will be created, therefore in the example Pass Type ID above, the description **Generic** is used.

13. The Identifier has to start with `pass.`, then a reverse domain name string is suggested, with the type of Pass placed on the end. In the example above, I use the full app ID created earlier, with Pass Type of generic, giving the full Pass Type Identifier as follows:

```
pass.pro.passkit.example.generic
```

With the Pass Type ID created, we will generate an associated cryptographic key and certificate, which is needed for authentication of the Pass. Select the Pass Type ID and note down the Pass Type ID, as this will be needed later when creating the Pass:

14. Click on the **Settings** button and follow the instructions to create a Certificate Signing Request. I will repeat the instructions below, with some suggestions to help avoid confusion later.

15. Launch the Keychain Access utility.

16. From the menu, select **Keychain Access | Certificate Assistant | Request a Certificate from a Certificate Authority**. In the **Certificate Information** window, enter the following:

   ❑ **User Email Address**: Enter the e-mail address associated with your iOS developer account.

   ❑ **Common Name**: Choose a name that relates to the Pass Type ID. This will be displayed next to the key in Keychain Access, so a common name that isn't specific enough can cause confusion. See the following screenshot, which is how this will be presented in Keychain Access after step 18.

> ❏ **CA Email Address**: Leave this field blank
>
> ❏ **Request is**: Choose **Saved to Disk**

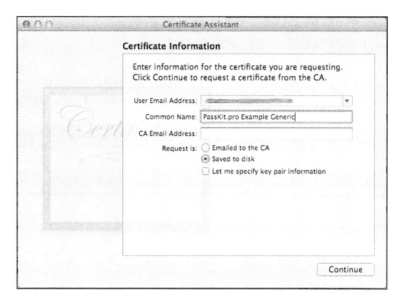

17. Click on **Continue** and save your Certificate Signing Request. Then, in Safari (other browsers may have problems or incompatibilities that prevent you from choosing a file), click on **Choose File** and select the Certificate Signing Request that has just been generated. Click on **Generate** and wait for the pass Type certificate to be generated:

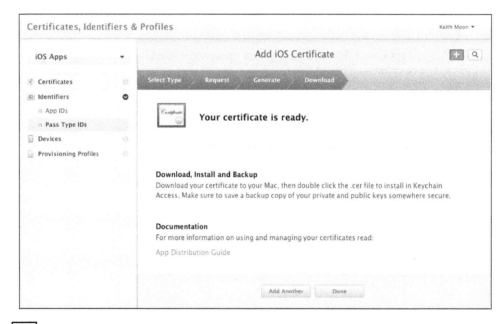

18. Once generated, click on **Done** and download your certificate. Open your downloaded certificate, which will launch Keychain Access and attach the certificate to the associated private key, which was created during the generation of the Certificate Signing Request:

The certificate and key pair should now be visible in Keychain Access. These now need to be converted into a format that can be used to correctly sign the Passes you will create. Select the certificate in Keychain Access, and from the menu choose **File | Export Items**, and choose an export location. You will be asked to provide a password to protect the exported items, you may also be asked for the administrator password as you are performing a task that requires administrator privileges.

You will need to use a command-line tool called OpenSSL to use the exported file to generate the key and certificate files that will be needed. This command line tool can be run from a built-in OSXutility called **Terminal**. To open Terminal, go to your `Applications` folder in `Finder`. Terminal is located in the `Utilities` folder.

1. Use the following Terminal commands to generate a `certificate.pem` file and a `key.pem` file.

   ```
   openssl pkcs12 -in <Path to exported .p12> -clcerts -nokeys -out
   certificate.pem

   openssl pkcs12 -in <Path to exported .p12> -nocerts -out key.pem
   ```

2. On generating the `key.pem`, you will be prompted to enter an import passport, which is the password that was set when exporting from Keychain Access. You will then be prompted for a pass phrase; this can be the same as the import password, but note that this pass phrase will need to provided when signing your Passes and so may form part of an automated script.

3. In addition to the `certificate.pem` file and `key.pem` file generated above, the Apple WWDR intermediate certificate is also required. This can be found by going to the provisioning portal, in the **Certificates** section, click on the **+** button, or visit the following. The certificate is labeled *Worldwide Developer Relations Certificate Authority* under Intermediate Certificates.

   ```
   https://developer.apple.com/account/ios/certificate/
   certificateCreate.action
   ```

4. Once this has been downloaded, it also needs to be converted into a `.pem` file. Double-click on the WWDR certificate file, to load it into Keychain Access, and select the certificate in Keychain Access:

| Apple Worldwide Developer Relations Certification Authority | certificate |

5. Then, from the menu choose **File | Export Items**, change the file format to **Privacy Enhanced Mail** (.pem) and save as it wwdr.pem.

How it works...

Apple's security model ensures that only registered iOS developers can create Passes and that Passes cannot be altered by a third party while being delivered to a user's device, without being detected, and rejected by Passbook.

The certificate creation process produces a Pass Type certificate that is tied to the Pass Type ID that it was created from, which in turn ties it to your developer account. This provides a method for verifying the contents of a Pass signed using this certificate, and therefore, a way of detecting any manipulation of the Pass by anyone other than the registered Pass creator.

Creating your Pass (Medium)

Passes are built and customized by specifying the relevant information in JSON format. Certain graphical assets can also be provided to further customize the look and feel of the Pass.

As an example, we will build a Pass of a Generic type, to be used as an employee identification card. Once we understand the JSON structure of this type, we will see how other Pass types differ.

Getting ready

You can get the full JSON code, which we will use, from the following link:

http://passkit.pro/example-generic-json

This will create a Pass that looks like the following two images.

The following screenshot shows the front of the Pass:

The back of the Pass is shown in the following screenshot:

How to do it...

1. Save the following JSON code to a file called `pass.json`:

```json
{
"passTypeIdentifier" : "pass.pro.passkit.example.generic",
  "formatVersion" : 1,
  "teamIdentifier" : "YAXJZJ267E",
  "organizationName" : "Passbook Example Company",
  "serialNumber" : "0000001",
  "description" : "Staff Pass for Employee Number 001",
  "associatedStoreIdentifiers" : [
    375380948
  ],
  "locations" : [
    {
  "latitude" : 51.50506,
  "longitude" : -0.01960,
  "relevantText" : "Company Offices"
}
  ],
  "foregroundColor" : "rgb(255, 255, 255)",
  "backgroundColor" : "rgb(90, 90, 90)",
  "labelColor" : "rgb(255, 255, 255)",
  "logoText" : "Company Staff ID",
  "barcode" : {
    "format" : "PKBarcodeFormatQR",
    "message" : "0000001",
    "messageEncoding" : "iso-8859-1",
    "altText" : "Staff ID 0000001"
  },
  "generic" : {
    "headerFields" : [
      {
        "key" : "staffNumber",
"label" : "Staff Number",
"value" : "001"
      }
    ],
  "primaryFields" : [
    {
  "key" : "staffName",
  "label" : "Name",
  "value" : "Peter Brooke"
}
    ],
  "secondaryFields" : [
```

```
{
"key" : "telephoneExt",
"label" : "Extension",
"value" : "9779"
},
{
"key" : "jobTitle",
"label" : "Job Title",
"value" : "Chief Pass Creator"
}
],
"backFields" : [
{
"key" : "managersName",
"label" : "Manager's Name",
"value" : "Paul Bailey"
},
{
"key" : "managersExt",
"label" : "Manager's Extension",
"value" : "9673"
},
{
"key" : "expiryDate",
"dateStyle" : "PKDateStyleShort",
"label" : "Expiry Date",
"value" : "2013-12-31T00:00-23:59"
}
]
}
}
```

2. Replace the value for `passTypeIdentifier` (currently `pass.pro.passkit.example.generic`) with your own Pass Type Identifier created previously.

3. Replace the value for `teamIdentifier` (currently `YAXJZJ267E`) with your own Team Identifier, noted previously as the App ID Prefix.

4. A number of graphical assets can be added to further customise the Pass. The only required graphical asset is an icon, which is used when displaying the Pass on the lock screen.

5. Create an icon for retina screens with dimensions of 58 px by 58 px, this should be named `icon@2x.png`. Create a non-retina version with dimensions 29 px by 29 px, this should be named `icon.png`. Example assets can downloaded from `http://passkit.pro/example-generic-package`.

How it works...

The `pass.json` file we've just created contains the following top-level key/value pairs:

- ▶ `passTypeIdentifier`: This ties the Pass to your developer account.

- ▶ `formatVersion`: Currently this is always 1, but it will allow Apple to vary the format in the future, while maintaining backwards compatibility.

- ▶ `teamIdentifier`: This identifier allows separate apps, by the same developer, to share data through the iOS keychain. For our purposes, this just needs to match the App ID Prefix specified when the Pass Type Identifier was created.

- ▶ `organizationName`: This is the name of your company or app, this should be how your users know and refer to you. It will be displayed as the title of the notification when a Pass is presented on the lock screen.

- ▶ `serialNumber`: This should contain a unique reference to the Pass, when updating a Pass, this serial number will be used to request the updated information from your server, and therefore this should uniquely identify only one Pass of this type. In the example of a staff identification Pass, this could be the employee reference number. While it's represented as a number in the example, it can be any text value.

- ▶ `description`: Used for accessibility features and so should briefly describe the Pass's use and should include enough information to distinguish it from other Passes of the same type.

- ▶ `associatedStoreIdentifiers`: An array of iTunes Store App Identifiers for Apps that are associated with this Pass. If you already have an app in the App Store, through which Passes will be provided, this should be included. An app's identifier can be found in iTunes Connect. If multiple identifiers are provided, the first one that is available for the device is used. This will present an App information banner on the back of the Pass. This banner will prompt the user to install your app or open the app if it is already installed.

The following two top-level key/value pairs determine under what circumstances the Pass is presented to the user on their lock screen.

- ▶ `locations`: This is a list of locations that are relevant to the use of the Pass. This is represented as an array of dictionaries containing the location information. Only one location is provided in the example, however up to 10 may be specified. If the user is within a certain distance of this location, they may be presented with the Pass on their lock screen. The distance from the location that triggers this behavior varies depending on the Pass type, for a generic Pass type the distance is approximately 100 meters. Each `locations` dictionary contains latitude, longitude, and relevant text that will be displayed on the lock screen when triggered. In the `locations` dictionary you can optionally specify altitude as well.

- ▸ `relevantDate`: Not included in the example above, as it didn't fit with the employer ID use case. This determines a time period within which the Pass is relevant. The value for this key should be text in the form of a W3C timestamp, for example, "2013-12-31T00:00-23:59", and can also include seconds if necessary. No timezone information should be included, as the timezone set in the device's settings is used.

The behavior of the two relevancy keys described above varies depending on the Pass type. The Pass type determines that for `locations` and `relevantDate`, which are required and which are options, it also determines the triggering criteria used in presenting a Pass on the user's lock screen.

An explanation of the differing behavior can be found in Apple's Passbook Programming Guide (Apple Developer account signin required) at:

```
https://developer.apple.com/library/ios/#documentation/
UserExperience/Conceptual/PassKit_PG/Chapters/Creating.html#//apple_
ref/doc/uid/TP40012195-CH4-SW53
```

- ▸ `foregroundColor`: The foreground color of the Pass, value provided as an RGB triple.

- ▸ `backgroundColor`: The background color of the Pass, value provided as an RGB triple.

- ▸ `labelColor`: The color of the text displayed in the Pass, value provided as an RGB triple.

- ▸ `logoText`: The text shown in the top-left hand corner of the Pass. This will mostly likely be the name of your company, or an indication of the Pass's use.

- ▸ `barcode`: This dictionary contains the information to display in a barcode and how to display it. The Pass format supports automatic creation of 2D barcodes in one of the following formats:

    - ❏ `PKBarcodeFormatQR`

    - ❏ `PKBarcodeFormatPDF417`

    - ❏ `PKBarcodeFormatAztec`

Message encoding will typically be `iso-8859-1`, unless you know that another encoding format is supported by your barcode scanner.

The value to be encoded into the barcode should be defined with the message key and the `altText` key used to optionally display a more human readable description of the barcode information.

▶ **generic**: This top-level key determines the type of Pass that you will be creating. The types currently available are:

- ❑ `generic`
- ❑ `boardingPass`
- ❑ `coupon`
- ❑ `eventTicket`
- ❑ `storeCard`

Your choice of Pass type effects many things about the Pass, including overall style, text layout, available graphical asset options, and lock screen behavior. Apple has optimized the Pass types for their individual use cases, so try to pick a Pass type that most closely represents your Pass's use case. If none of the specific Pass types are appropriate, then the generic Pass type can be used.

The Passbook Programming Guide describes the different layout configurations for each Pass type:

```
https://developer.apple.com/library/ios/#documentation/
UserExperience/Conceptual/PassKit_PG/Chapters/Creating.html#//apple_
ref/doc/uid/TP40012195-CH4-SW1
```

Within the Pass type top-level key is a dictionary, containing arrays of various display groups, including `headerFields`, `primaryFields`, `secondaryFields`, and `backFields`, which are displayed according to Pass type. Each group contains an array of dictionaries, specifying key, label, and value. The label and value fields are displayed on the Pass, while the key field should be unique within your Pass format, and will be used when updating a Pass.

There's more...

Graphical assets can be provided to further visually customize your Pass. The `icon.png` asset is required, but the following assets can optionally be included in the Pass package:

- ▶ `logo.png`
- ▶ `background.png`
- ▶ `thumbnail.png`
- ▶ `footer.png`
- ▶ `strip.png`

All assets should include a retina version that is twice as wide and twice as high, with @2x at the end of the filename. Therefore, for the icon, you provide the following files:

- `icon.png`: 29 px width x 29 px height
- `icon@2x.png`: 58 px width x 58 px height

The following table provides the available size of each asset, and the space available for each Pass type. The sizes are provided as pixels width x pixels height:

Pass Type	icon 29 x 29	logo 160 x 50	background 180 x 220	thumbnail 90 x 90*	strip **	footer 286x15
Generic	Required	Optional	Not used	Optional	Not used	Not used
Boarding pass	Required	Optional	Not used	Not used	Not used	Optional
Coupon	Required	Optional	Not used	Not used	Optional	No
Event ticket	Required	Optional	Optional	Optional	Not used	Not used
(with strip)			Not used	Not used	Optional	
Store card	Required	Optional	Not used	Not used	Optional	Not used

* 90px x 90px is the space available, but the graphic must be either 60px x 90px, or 90px x 60px

** Allowed size for the strip asset is 312 x 84 for Event tickets, 312 x 110 when a square barcode is used and 312 x 123 otherwise.

Further documentation

Further details of Pass type layout structures can be found in the Apple Passbook Package Format Reference (Apple Developer account signin required) at:

```
https://developer.apple.com/library/ios/#documentation/
UserExperience/Reference/PassKit_Bundle/Chapters/Introduction.html#//
apple_ref/doc/uid/TP40012026
```

Signing your Pass (Simple)

Now that you have built and customized your Pass, you will need to digitally sign the Pass package contents, so that it will be accepted by the Passbook app.

We will make use of the certificate and keys generated previously. This will sign the Pass with your developer identity, allowing your Pass to be validated and used with the Passbook app:

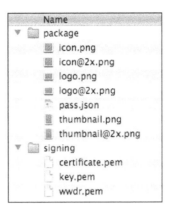

Getting ready

The graphical assets for your Pass and the `pass.json` file should be in their own folder, with the `.pem` files created earlier, in a higher level folder.

Here is an example of the folder structure:

How to do it...

1. Save the following JSON code into a file called `manifest.json`.

```
{
    "pass.json":"4f5cef0afe8171f736de367b202ca054abfb3663",
    "icon.png":"8c58c1fbf11f944c03b5cd5e41dc6d301263c1f7",
    "icon@2x.png":"ae3395b5e252610b02d51d52a534c700837ced2d"
}
```

2. This file should contain a JSON dictionary, where each key is the filename of a contained in your Pass package, and the value is the SHA1 hash of that file. To determine the SHA1 value, open your Terminal App, and enter the following commands:

```
cd [Path to the folder containing the Pass package]
opensslsha1 *
```

3. Place the resulting hash values into the `manifest.json` file.

4. The manifest file then needs to be digitally signed, to produce a signature file, which will verify that the contents of the Pass have not been modified. This can be done using the following Terminal command. (Note that this requires administrator privileges, so you will need to enter your administrator password.):

```
sudo open sslsmime -binary -sign -certfile ../signing/wwdr.
pem -signer ../sgning/certificate.pem -inkey ../signing/key.pem
-in manifest.json -out signature -outform DER -passin pass:[Pass
phrase provided when creating the key.pem]
```

5. If your folder differs from the preceding suggestion, you will need to alter the paths to the `.pem` files accordingly.

6. Your package folder should now include:

   ❑ Graphical assets

   ❑ `pass.json`

   ❑ `manifest.json`

   ❑ The `signature` file

   Place the files in your package folder into a ZIP file. This can be done by selecting all the files and navigating to **File | Compress** from the **Finder** menu.

7. Rename the resulting ZIP file to change the file extension to `.pkpass`. If you have filenames set to be hidden, you may be changing the filename and not the extension. To show filename extensions, select **Finder | Preferences** from the menu and enable **Show all filename extensions**.

Congratulations! You now have a customized and signed Pass.

How it works...

The goal of the signing process is to prevent the Pass from being modified by a third party between leaving your servers and being received by the user. When the `manifest.json` file is created, each file in the Pass package has its hash value calculated and stored. If the contents of any of the files were to change, its hash value would also change, therefore this `manifest.json` file represents an easy way of checking that the Pass package files have not been modified.

However, this on it's own is not enough, as a third party could modify the `manifest.json` file when they modify other files in the package. To guard against this, public/private key encryption is used to produce a signature file from the `manifest.json`. Your private key, to which only you have access, was used to generate the file, but anyone with access to the public key can use it to verify that the manifest file hasn't been tampered with.

Using this process, the user's device can be sure that the source of the Pass it receives is genuine and hasn't been altered in transit.

Because of this verification, it is important that only files specified in the `manifest.json` file are included in the zipped file. Individually selecting the files in Finder, and then choosing compress from the menu, is a good way to ensure this. Be careful if you choose to zip the entire contents of a folder, possibly through a Terminal command, as this can include additional hidden files like `.DS_Store`.

Changing the file extension tells the system that it should be treated as a Pass instead of a regular ZIP file.

There's more...

It's important to understand the process and steps involved in signing a Pass, however it is unlikely that it will be feasible to manually perform these steps for every Pass that you create. Instead they should form part of an automated system for producing your user's Passes.

Pre-built Pass creation implementations are starting to emerge, including this PHPserver code:

`https://github.com/tschoffelen/PHP-Passkit`

Delivering your Pass via e-mail (Medium)

Passes can be delivered as an e-mail attachment, allowing the recipient to view the Pass and add it to their Passbook app.

Getting ready

The Pass e-mail creation script, used below, can be downloaded from the following location:

```
http://passkit.pro/ruby-email-script
```

How to do it...

1. Save the following code into a file named send_pass_by_email.rb.

```ruby
require 'net/smtp'

# This script accepts the following arguments: recipients name,
recipients email address, path to Pass.
# Example usage:
# ruby send_pass_by_email.rb "Peter Brooke" pbrooke@passkit.pro
../Pass-Example-Generic/Pass-Example-Generic.pkpass

# Retrieve command line arguments
recipientName = ARGV[0]
recipientEmail = ARGV[1]
passFilePath = ARGV[2]

# Setup template email values
senderName = "Passbook Example Company"
senderEmail = "info@passkit.pro"
emailSubjectText = "New Employee Pass"
emailBodyText = "Please find attached your new employee Pass"

# Setup SMTP settings
smtpDomain = "TO DEFINE. Eg. gmail.com"
smtpLogin = "TO DEFINE. Eg. ......@gmail.com"
smtpPassword = "TO DEFINE"

# Read file and base64 encode
fileContent = File.read(passFilePath)
encodedContent = [fileContent].pack("m")
```

```
# The is used to separate the MIME parts, it can be anything
# as long as it does not appear elsewhere in the email text
boundaryMarker = "SEPARATINGSTRINGNOTFOUNDELSEWHERE"

# Setup the email headers.
headers =<<EOF
From: #{senderName} <#{senderEmail}>
To: #{recipientName} <#{recipientEmail}>
Subject: #{emailSubjectText}
MIME-Version: 1.0
Content-Type: multipart/mixed; boundary=#{boundaryMarker}
--#{boundaryMarker}
EOF

# Setup the email body
body =<<EOF
Content-Type: text/plain
Content-Transfer-Encoding:8bit

#{emailBodyText}
--#{boundaryMarker}
EOF

# Setup the Pass attachment with the correct MIME Encoding
attachment =<<EOF
Content-Type: application/vnd.apple.pkpass;
name=\"#{passFilePath}\"
Content-Transfer-Encoding:base64
Content-Disposition: attachment; filename="#{passFilePath}"

#{encodedContent}
--#{boundaryMarker}--
EOF

completeEmail = headers + body + attachment

# Send email using your SMTP settings
smtp = Net::SMTP.new 'smtp.gmail.com', 587
smtp.enable_starttls
smtp.start(smtpDomain, smtpLogin, smtpPassword, :login) do
  smtp.send_message(completeEmail, senderEmail, recipientEmail)
end
```

2. Under the section headed **# Setup template email values**, enter relevant values for the sender name, sender e-mail address, subject, and e-mail body.

3. Under the section header **# Setup SMTP settings**, enter the details of the SMTP e-mail server and account details that will be used to send the e-mail. These can be found from the setting of your e-mail client, or you can use a free e-mail service like Gmail.

4. This Ruby script accepts three arguments, the recipient's name, the recipient's e-mail address and the path to the Pass to be attached. Open the Terminal and send a Pass-enabled e-mail by calling the script with appropriate arguments, as shown in the following example:

```
ruby <Path to send_pass_by_email.rb> "Peter Brooke" pbrooke@
passkit.pro <Path to Pass to attach .pkpass>
```

The following screenshot shows what the resulting e-mail will look like on iOS:

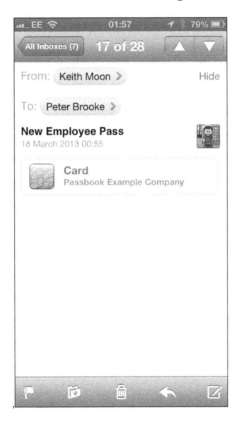

5. If you sent this e-mail to an e-mail account you have access to, open this e-mail in the Mail app on an iPhone running iOS 6 or Mail on OSX 10.8.2, and you will be given the option to open and view the Pass and add it to Passbook.

How it works...

The script used above is written in Ruby, as the Ruby interpreter is installed by default on OSX.

Sending a Pass as an attachment that will be understood by iOS and OSX, and presented to the user, requires it to have a specific MIME Type specified in the attachment. This MIME type is the following:

application/vnd.apple.pkpass

This script, or something similar could be used to automate the delivery of Passes to a large number of users, through email.

Delivering your Pass via a web link (Medium)

You can deliver a Pass to your users by linking to it from your website, for instance, from a confirmation page.

Getting ready

You will need access to your own web server, or shared hosting space with FTP access. The following instructions are for an Apache web server. Mac OSX does come with an Apache web server built in, which can be used. This used to be available under the **Sharing** menu in **System Preferences**, however since OSX 10.8 it can only be activated by the command line. You can run the following command from the Terminal, to start the web server:

```
sudoapachectl start
```

The root for this server can be found at `/Library/WebServer/Documents/`.

The files we will create can be downloaded from the following location:

```
http://passkit.pro/apache-mime-type
```

How to do it...

1. Save the following MIME type instruction into a file named `htaccess`:
   ```
   AddType application/vnd.apple.pkpass pkpass
   ```

2. Create an HTML page linking to a Pass, shown as follows , and save it as `index.html`:
   ```
   Get your employee pass <a href='Pass-Example-Generic.
   pkpass'>HERE</a>
   ```

3. Upload your `htaccess` file, the `index.html` file and the Pass file to a publicly accessible directory on your web sever. If you are running your web server locally, place these files within the web server's root folder.

4. Rename the `htaccess` file to `.htaccess`. (The file may disappear, as files starting with a `.` are treated as hidden files.)

5. With Mobile Safari on your iPhone, visit the URL for the `index.html` file on your web server.

6. Follow the link to your Pass and Mobile Safari will display the Pass so it can be added to Passbook.

How it works...

For the Safari or Mobile Safari browser to understand a Pass file and display it to the user, your Web server needs to present the files with the MIME type of `application/vnd.apple.pkpass`.

The `.htaccess` file tells the web server how to treat files in the folder in which resides. In this case it is instructing the web server to inform any visiting web browser that files with the file extension `pkpass` are to be treated as Passes. The `.htaccess` must be placed in each folder that contains a Pass.

Only users of a browser that supports this MIME type will be present with the Pass dialog, the rest will be prompted to download the Pass. While Safari and Mobile Safari support Passes, other third party browsers may not. However, the current versions of Chrome on iOS and the in-app browser from the Facebook app do support Pass display.

There's more...

If you wish to add server-wide support of the Pass MIME type, you can add an entry to your Apache web server's `mimes.type` file, this is located in the `conf` directory. Open up the file in a text editor and add the following line in the correct alphabetical position:

```
application/vnd.apple.pkpass pkpass
```

You will need to restart the server for this to take effect.

Delivering your Pass via an app (Medium)

Passes can be delivered through a companion iOS app. The app will provide a UI, using Apple's PassKit framework, allowing the user to view a Pass and choose to add it to their Passbook.

Getting ready

To follow these steps, it is assumed that you have some experience of Objective-C and creating iOS apps.

The example project, created as follows, can be downloaded from the following location:

```
http://passkit.pro/example-app
```

This app does not use **Automatic Reference Counting** (**ARC**), if you are using the code in an ARC environment, remove any calls to releasing objects.

How to do it...

1. Open Xcode and create a new, single view project. The setup options used for the example project are shown in the following screenshot:

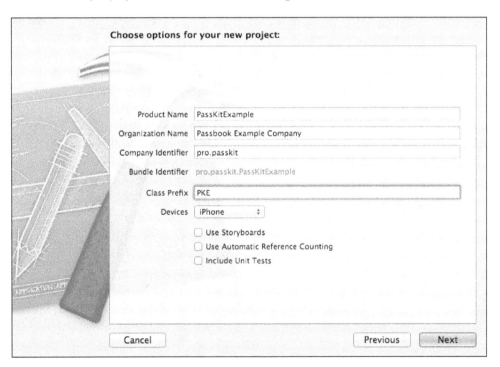

2. In the Target settings, under **Build Phases**, expand the **Link Binaries With Libraries** section, and click on the **+** button. Search for the PassKit framework and add it. After this, the list of linked libraries should look like this:

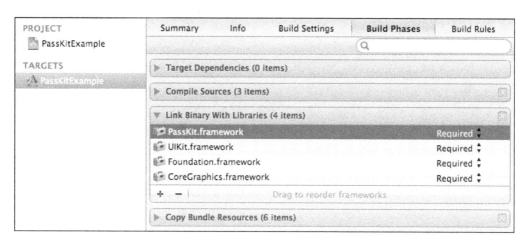

3. Add your previously created Pass to the project by dragging the file to the project navigator, in the example, this Pass is called `Pass-Example-Generic.pkpass`.

    In **PKEViewController.h**, replace the existing code with the following:

    ```
    #import <UIKit/UIKit.h>
    #import <PassKit/PassKit.h>


    @interface PKEViewController : UIViewController<PKAddPassesViewCon
    trollerDelegate>


    @property (nonatomic, retain) IBOutletUIButton *addPassButton;


    - (IBAction)addPassButtonPressed:(id)sender;


    @end
    ```

4. In **PKEViewController.m** replace the existing code with the following:

    ```
    #import "PKEViewController.h"


    @interface PKEViewController ()


    @property (nonatomic, retain) PKPass *genericPass;


    @end


    @implementation PKEViewController
    ```

```objc
- (void)viewDidLoad
{
    [super viewDidLoad];
  // Do any additional setup after loading the view, typically
from a nib.

    // Create the PKPass from the bundled file
    // In a real App this may be retrive from the network.

NSString *passFilePath = [[NSBundle mainBundle]
pathForResource:@"Pass-Example-Generic" ofType:@"pkpass"];
NSData *passData = [[NSDataalloc] initWithContentsOfFile:passFileP
ath];
NSError *passError;
    _genericPass = [[PKPass alloc] initWithData:passData
error:&passError];
    [passData release];

}


- (void)didReceiveMemoryWarning
{
    [super didReceiveMemoryWarning];
    // Dispose of any resources that can be recreated.
}

- (void)dealloc {

    [_addPassButton release];
    [_genericPass release];

    [super dealloc];
}

#pragma mark - IBAction Methods

- (IBAction)addPassButtonPressed:(id)sender {

    if (![PKPassLibrary isPassLibraryAvailable]) {

NSLog(@"Passbook not available on this device");
        return;

    }
```

```objc
PKAddPassesViewController *addPassViewController =
[[PKAddPassesViewController alloc] initWithPass:self.genericPass];
addPassViewController.delegate = self;

    [self presentViewController:addPassViewController animated:YES
completion:^{

  NSLog(@"Add Pass view controller presented");

    }];

    [addPassViewController release];
}

#pragma mark - PKAddPassesViewControllerDelegate Methods

- (void)addPassesViewControllerDidFinish:(PKAddPassesViewControll
er *)controller {

    // Check if the Pass is now in the Pass Library

PKPassLibrary *passLibrary = [[PKPassLibrary alloc] init];

    if ([passLibrary containsPass:self.genericPass]) {

        // If the Pass is now in the Library, we can't re-add it,
only view it.
        [self.addPassButton setTitle:@"View Pass in Passbook"
forState:UIControlStateNormal];

    }

    [self dismissViewControllerAnimated:YES completion:^{

  NSLog(@"Add Pass view controller dismissed");

    }];

}

@end
```

Open **PKEViewController.xib**, place a `UIButton` with the title **Add Pass to Passbook** on the view and connect it to `IBOutlet` **addPassButton** and IBAction**addPassButtonPressed** for the sent event Touch Up Inside:

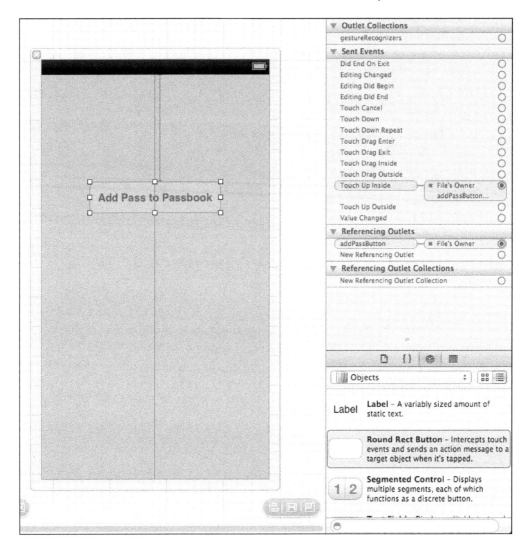

5. Run the project in the iPhone Simulator. Tapping on the **Add Pass To Passbook** button will launch the PassKit UI, which displays the Pass and would allow the user to add the Pass to the Passbook app. At this stage however, the Pass will not be successfully added to the Passbook app as we need to use the correct provisioning profile.

6. To build the app to an iPhone, we will need an appropriate provisioning profile. Therefore, you need to log in to the Apple Developer Center:

   `https://developer.apple.com/account/ios/profile/profileList.action`

7. Under **Provisioning**, click on the **New Profile** button, and follow these steps:

8. Choose a name for the development profile.

9. Tick next to your certificate.

10. Select the App ID in which you enabled Passes and generated certificates for previously.

11. Choose the devices you will be using.

12. Click on **Submit**.

13. Once generated, download the provisioning profile and open it to load it into Xcode.

14. In **Target** settings, under **Info**, ensure that the Bundle Identifier matches the app ID that was previously created and chosen in the profile creation.

15. In **Build Settings**, under **Code Signing Identity**, ensure the profile created above is selected under **Debug**.

16. Build to the device, and test that the presented Pass is successfully added to Passbook.

How it works...

The example app uses the PassKit framework to present a framework supplied view controller to the user, listen for a delegate callback when the user finishes interacting with the view controller and changes the button's title if the Pass was successfully added to Passbook.

Using the following code, the PKPass object is created from a NSData object:

```
NSString *passFilePath = [[NSBundle mainBundle]
pathForResource:@"Pass-Example-Generic" ofType:@"pkpass"];
NSData *passData = [[NSDataalloc] initWithContentsOfFile:passFilePa
th];
NSError *passError;
_genericPass = [[PKPassalloc] initWithData:passData error:&passError];
[passData release];
```

For the sake of simplicity, in this example, the Pass is loaded from a file bundled with the app. It is much more likely in a real-world app that a Pass will be downloaded from a network resource.

`PKPassLibrary` provides access to the Passes contained in Passbook. It also provides a class method called `isPassLibraryAvailable` that will tell you if Passbook exists on that device, for example Passbook is not present on iPads. This method is used in the example app to decide whether to show the Pass view controller.

```
if (![PKPassLibrary isPassLibraryAvailable]) {
    NSLog(@"Passbook not available on this device");
    return;
}
```

There's more...

Further documentation of the PassKit framework can be found in the following location:

```
https://developer.apple.com/library/ios/#documentation/
UserExperience/Reference/PassKit_Framework/
```

Updating a Pass within the Passbook app (Advanced)

Apple provides a mechanism for updating a Pass that has been added to Passbook by a user. This process involves sending a push notification to the user's device, and implementing a REST API that will respond to the device's requests and provide the relevant updated Pass information.

Getting ready

The first stage in updating a Pass is to send a Push Notification to the user's device to prompt the Pass update process. The process for sending **Apple Push Notifications** (**APNs**) is outside the scope for this book, and the assumption will made that the facility to send the appropriate APN is available. Further information on APNs can be found in Apple's documentation:

```
https://developer.apple.com/library/ios/#documentation/
NetworkingInternet/Conceptual/RemoteNotificationsPG/Introduction/
Introduction.html
```

In implementing the required REST API, we will be making use of the GIT source control management tool. If you don't already have GIT installed and setup, follow the GitHub tutorial:

```
https://help.github.com/articles/set-up-git
```

How to do it...

1. Open Terminal and change the directory to the directory that is to contain the server code.

2. We will be using the open source example Passbook server built in Ruby on Rails by Mattt Thompson (`https://github.com/mattt`), so we first need to clone the server code from the repository, with the following command:

   ```
   git clone https://github.com/keefmoon/passbook_rails_example.git
   ```

3. You will need to install Xcode command-line tools, you can do this by opening Xcode and on the menu, going to **Xcode | Preferences | Download** and clicking on **Install** next to **Command Line Tools**.

4. Change to the directory containing the code and prepare the Ruby App:

   ```
   cd passbook_rails_example
   bundle
   ```

5. If you get an error related to Postgres, use the following command to install it separately and run the `bundle` command again. (This command will require administrator access.)

   ```
   sudo env ARCHFLAGS="-arch x86_64" gem install pg
   ```

6. Depending on the version of Ruby installed, you may have an extra command to enter. Mountain Lion comes bundled with Ruby 1.8.7 and will require the extra command, but if you have updated to version 1.9.2 or greater, then the following command is not required. (Administration access will be required.):

   ```
   sudo gem installrdoc-data
   sudo rdoc-data --install
   ```

7. Open [path to server code]`/db/seeds.rb` in a text editor. The content in this file will be used to populate the database initially, therefore replace the example data with details that match your previously created Pass, ensure that the pass type identifier and serial number are correct, but change at least one part of the Pass data. In the following example, I have changed Peter Brooke's job title from `Chief Pass Creator`, to `CTO`.

   ```
   pass = Passbook::Pass.create(pass_type_identifier: "pass.
   pro.passkit.example.generic", serial_number: "0000001",
   authentication_token: "UniqueAuthTokenABCD1234")
   pass.data = {
   ```

```
        staffName: "Peter Brooke",
        telephoneExt: "9779",
        jobTitle: "CTO",
        managersName: "Paul Bailey",
        managersExt: "9673",
        expiryDate: "2013-12-31T00:00-23:59"
    }
    pass.save

    pass.registrations.create(device_library_identifier: "123456789",
    push_token: "00000000 00000000 00000000 00000000 00000000 00000000
    00000000 00000000")
```

8. In the `seeds.rb` file, specify a unique authentication token for each Pass you add. in the preceding example **UniqueAuthTokenABCD1234** is used, although this would be automatically generated in a real-world use.

9. Deploying this server code to the free Heroku service is the quickest and easiest way to make it available for testing. Visit `http://www.heroku.com` and sign up for an account.

10. Download and install the HerokuToolbelt for OSX:

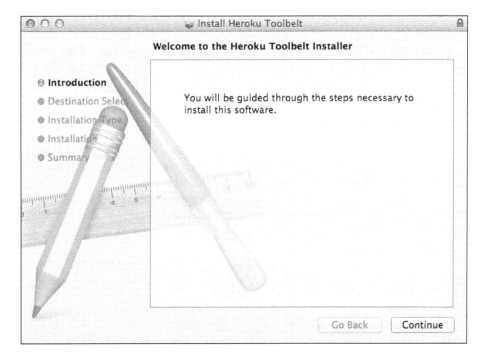

11. Open Terminal and log in to Heroku. Then create a new Heroku App and push the server code to it. Heroku will generate a name for your App; for example `http://frozen-bayou-9500.herokuapp.com/`.

```
heroku create
git push heroku master
heroku run rake db:createdb:migratedb:seed
```

12. For the Passes we have previously created to update using the server, we need to include the relevant information in the Pass. (In the following code sample, note that the sample web server has the additional path component of `passbook` in the `webServiceURL`.) Open the `pass.json` previously created and add two top-level keys with the relevant values, reproduce the `manifest.json`, reproduce the `signature` file, and re-zip the package files.

```
"authenticationToken" : "UniqueAuthTokenABCD1234",
"webServiceURL" : "http://frozen-bayou-9500.herokuapp.com/
passbook",
```

How it works...

The server we have implemented above is to facilitate the Pass update process, which involves back and forth communication between the user's device and your server.

When a user adds a Pass to Passbook that contains `webServiceURL` and `authenticationToken` keys, the device registers with your server, passing a device library ID that is used to authenticate further communication, the authentication token to authenticate this initial communication, and a push token to be used when sending an APN.

When information contained in the Pass changes, in our example this may be Peter Brooke being promoted, your server sends an APN to the device, using the push token it received. (The sending of this push notification is outside the scope of this book.) This prompts the device to ask your server for a list of all the updated Passes since it last asked. From this list, the device asks for updated information for each of the Passes in turn. Finally, the server responds with the updated Pass information and the updated Pass is presented to the user.

There's more...

Further information on the Pass update process can be found in the Apple documentation:

`https://developer.apple.com/library/ios/#documentation/
UserExperience/Conceptual/PassKit_PG/Chapters/Updating.html`

There is also a full specification for the REST API that the server above implements:

`https://developer.apple.com/library/ios/#documentation/PassKit/
Reference/PassKit_WebService/WebService.html`

When testing the web service endpoints in a browser, it is necessary to include the following request header in addition to any authorization header described in the specification:

```
Accept: application/json
```

In a live production setting, the web service must use HTTPS, however you can allow Passbook on your device to use HTTP for development testing. If your device has been enabled for development using Xcode, you will have an additional **Developer** section under the app settings . In the **Developer** section, under **PassKit Testing**, switch on **Allow HTTP Services**:

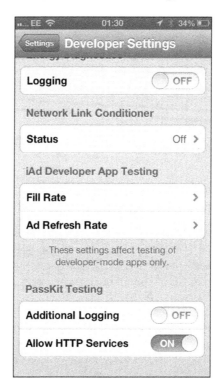

About Packt Publishing

Packt, pronounced 'packed', published its first book "*Mastering phpMyAdmin for Effective MySQL Management*" in April 2004 and subsequently continued to specialize in publishing highly focused books on specific technologies and solutions.

Our books and publications share the experiences of your fellow IT professionals in adapting and customizing today's systems, applications, and frameworks. Our solution based books give you the knowledge and power to customize the software and technologies you're using to get the job done. Packt books are more specific and less general than the IT books you have seen in the past. Our unique business model allows us to bring you more focused information, giving you more of what you need to know, and less of what you don't.

Packt is a modern, yet unique publishing company, which focuses on producing quality, cutting-edge books for communities of developers, administrators, and newbies alike. For more information, please visit our website: www.packtpub.com.

Writing for Packt

We welcome all inquiries from people who are interested in authoring. Book proposals should be sent to author@packtpub.com. If your book idea is still at an early stage and you would like to discuss it first before writing a formal book proposal, contact us; one of our commissioning editors will get in touch with you.

We're not just looking for published authors; if you have strong technical skills but no writing experience, our experienced editors can help you develop a writing career, or simply get some additional reward for your expertise.

PUBLISHING

PhoneGap 2.x Mobile
Application Development
Hotshot

ISBN: 978-1-849519-40-3   Paperback: 388 pages

Create exciting apps for mobile devices using PhoneGap

1. Ten apps included to help you get started on
   your very own exciting mobile app.

2. These apps include working with localization,
   social networks, geolocation, as well as the
   camera, audio, video, plugins, and more.

3. Apps cover the spectrum from productivity apps,
   educational apps, all the way to entertainment
   and games.

4. Many exciting and engaging suggestions that
   you can use to improve your apps.

Instant Apple Configurator
How-to

ISBN: 978-1-849694-06-3   Paperback: 88 pages

Gain full control and complete security when managing
mobile iOS devices in mass deployments

1. Learn something new in an Instant! A short,
   fast, focused guide delivering immediate results.

2. Configure group settings to personalize and
   secure your devices.

3. Deploy multiple profiles.

4. Upload and manage mass applications swiftly
   and easily.

Please check **www.PacktPub.com** for information on our titles

Instant New iPad Features in iOS 6 How-to

ISBN: 978-1-782160-46-5   Paperback: 74 pages

Learn to use Mail, iCloud, Photo Stream, iPhoto, iWorks, iTunes, iMovie, and Garageband through easy-to-follow recipes

1. Learn something new in an Instant! A short, fast, focused guide delivering immediate results.

2. Set up Mail using multiple accounts and a VIP Inbox.

3. Enable iCloud for synchronous use with other Apple devices and programs.

4. Understand Photostream and its key features.

iOS 5 Essentials

ISBN: 978-1-849692-26-7   Paperback: 252 pages

Harness iOS 5's new powerful features to create stunning applications

1. Integrate iCloud, Twitter, and AirPlay into your applications.

2. Lots of step-by-step examples, images, and diagrams to get you up to speed in no time with helpful hints along the way.

3. Each chapter explains iOS 5's new features in-depth, whilst providing you with enough practical examples to help incorporate these features in your apps.

Please check **www.PacktPub.com** for information on our titles

www.ingramcontent.com/pod-product-compliance
Lightning Source LLC
LaVergne TN
LVHW080105070326
832902LV00014B/2437